A
Northern
Woman

A
Northern
Woman

Jacqueline Baldwin

Caitlin Press Inc.
Prince George, B.C.

Published by
Caitlin Press Inc.
Box 2387
Prince George BC V2N 2S6

Design and typeset by Warren Clark Graphic Design

Caitlin Press acknowledges the financial support from Canada Council for the
Arts, The Candian Department of Heritage and the British Columbia Arts
Council for its publishing program.

BRITISH
COLUMBIA
ARTS COUNCIL
Supported by the Province of British Columbia

THE CANADA COUNCIL | LE CONSEIL DES A
FOR THE ARTS | DU CANADA
SINCE 1957 | DEPUIS 1957

National Library of Canada Cataloguing in Publication Data
Baldwin, Jacqueline, 1934-
   A Northern woman
   Poems

   ISBN 1-894759-01-X
   I. Title.   PS8553.A448N67 2003   C811'.54   C203-910850-3
PR9199.3.B353N67 2003

Acknowledgments

Some of the poems in this book have been published in journals and anthologies: *Reflections On Water; It's Still Winter; Chips From The Block Anthology; Beyond Grief Anthology; Writer's Bloc Anthology; The Federation of B.C. Writers 2003 Anthology* as well as in the magazines: *Interior B.C. Woman; Guide To The Goldfields; and Connections.*

"It Is Anna Whom We Mourn" has been exhibited on the walls of Art Space Gallery during International Women's Week, and "Call The Name Gently: Ne-chaaaaa-ko" was featured at the Two Rivers Art Gallery and published in their exhibit catalogue.

My grateful thanks to all those who encourage me in my writing, who attend my readings and write me beautiful letters about their lives, and their responses to my poems. Thanks to my editor, Cynthia Wilson, for her guidance and support of my work.

I feel fortunate to live in this extraordinary place in Northern British Columbia where enthusiasm, reciprocity, harmony, and an appreciation of diversity combine to provide a community where creative arts can flourish.

This book is dedicated to

the memory of my mother: Letitia Barbara Mackenzie Morse,
my grandmothers: Maggie Macaulay Mackenzie, of Oamaru, New
Zealand; and Selena Priscilla MacDonell Morse of Inverhoe, New
Zealand

to their mothers, my great-grandmothers: Ann Cameron MacDonell
and Catherine Macaulay

and to my Canadian grand-daughters:
Mackenzie Cathlynn Baldwin, and Macaulay Danielle Baldwin
who carry the songs and stories

INTRODUCTION

"*A Northern Woman*" blends a collection of narrative poems, prose poems, stories, and essays. The power of story intrigues and enchants me: especially in the way it shapes, heals, and teaches us about the world and our own lives. I like the process of bringing narrative and prose into poetry, bringing them closer together.

In "The Pine Trees Singing", I talk about the experience of living in a large extended family "*marinated in love and story,*" and how those stories - "yarns" they were called in New Zealand - grounded me and provided me with a sense of belonging on the earth.

Some of the stories and poetry recitations I listened to as a child introduced me to ancestors who were dead long years before I was born. I knew these characters well: their trials, triumphs, humour, courage, and heartbreaks. The narratives taught me about countries far away, and what New Zealand was like when the first settlers arrived. The stories were told, and heard, with great respect and regarded as a sacred trust. My passion to write, and my love for cadence, originated in those evening gatherings of people who held the value and ritual of oral storytelling in high esteem.

The book is divided into six chapters. *Aotearoa: Land Of The Long White Cloud* gathers work written about my life and family in New Zealand. Chapter Two: *Seven Thousand Rivers*, contains two poem/essays. In chapter three, my work addresses the realities of violence against women, under the heading: *Courage Of The Wild*

Crocus. Chapter Four: *Twelve Salmon Pink Roses* and Chapter Five: *Chaos And Delight* include poems that speak of the ironies of life, of relationships, and of the beauty and pain of motherhood and marriage. The final chapter: *Chiaroscuro: Clear Dark* is devoted to narrative poems about experiences, people, and adventures of life in Canada, in the unique landscape of Northern British Columbia.

Jacqueline Baldwin
Prince George
British Columbia
Canada
October 01, 2003.

Contents

1. Aotearoa: Land Of The Long White Cloud

2. Seven Thousand Rivers

3. Courage Of The Wild Crocus

4. Twelve Salmon Pink Roses

5. Chaos And Delight: The Melody Of What Happens

6. Chiaroscuro: Clear Dark

Aotearoa:
Land Of The Long White Cloud

Cotyledon

The Pine Trees Singing

December 5, 1911:
  The Night That Amy

Addendum
  [Afterword to December 5, 1911]

Marconi's Invention
  Does Not Please A Pre-Queen

Baling Wire, Fence Wire

Penultimate

Grand-dad Visits Canada

Responsibility

Beggars Would Ride

Swimming Against The Tide

Cotyledon

writing has a life of its own
won't take no for an answer

pushes itself through to the light
determined to reveal to the writer
an individual absolute truth

I trust this process
it's like dancing a path to the heart
painting your way home

The Pine Trees Singing

When I was a little girl, my grandmother Maggie used to tuck me into bed at night and create a circle of warmth and deep contentment with her air of promise about bedtime stories. She would say this: *"Listen, children, do you hear the sound of the pine trees singing? It is the wind, bringing stories. I'll put the lamp in the window."*

As I snuggled down in my warm bed, she would walk to the kitchen and light the kerosene lamp, then place it in the centre of the oilcloth covered table so that its light could be seen outside. When my grandfather walked up the hill toward the house in the gathering dusk after finishing the farm chores for the day, he would be guided by the lamp in the window, beaming its welcome through the four panes of glass. The feeling of anticipation for the stories that would later lull me to sleep, and the security of knowing that Granddad would soon be sitting in his chair at the kitchen table, drinking his tea and telling my grandmother the events of the evening, surrounded me with love and peace. She called the transition between daylight and dark "the gloaming." The gloaming, that time of great beauty, was a good friend to me, as beloved to me as the wind and the trees.

There were pine trees growing up the hill behind our house, and I often sat up there among them during the daytime, listening to the sound of their singing in the wind.

I knew just what she meant about the singing. It felt sacred, a textured presence, as if the trees knew that I was there, thinking about the stories. The sounds of the trees, singing, accompanied me always, their melodies a celebration of our allegiance. I imagined the trees gathering up the stories the wind brought, holding them in their branches until the lamp was in the window, and then the stories would magically transmit themselves to my beautiful Grandmother Maggie, so that she could tell them. Everything between the earth and the sky was mine; deeply loved, and intimately known. I could speak to everything without words, and in the same way, the sky and the wind, the trees and the gloaming would answer me. Down the hills below our house, beyond the lush green of the hedged farm fields, the shining waters of the Waitaki sent reassuring messages as the river flowed along on its journey from the Southern Alps to the Pacific Ocean.

I spent my early life marinated in deep love and in stories. I believed Maggie when she said:

"Listen children: do you hear the sound of the pine trees singing? It is the wind, bringing stories. I'll put the lamp in the window."

I believed her then. I believe her still.

December 5, 1911: The Night That Amy

eighteen miles to drive the
horse and buggy through the dark
Georgetown to Oamaru

the other little children
home with father

Maggie's ribs hurt from
holding her breath, listening
waiting for Amy to stop the terrible coughing
a rasping fierce enough to pierce the heart

urging the horse on
please god please keep me safe from
the big black watchdog at the station house
I've never driven in the night before
that dog terrifies me
even in the day time
jumping up and barking at everyone riding by
let alone in the pitch black with just a pale moon
he could jump right up over the wheels
frighten the horse and make her bolt
I have to get Amy to the doctor
she is so sick and we still have miles to go
please god please god
don't let that dog harm us

she spoke quietly under her breath
strong in her belief that if they could just
get past the big black dog safely
everything else would be all right

a hedge of marcrocarpa trees surrounded the station
Maggie peered through the moonlight
looking for a shadow that could become a dog
hoping he would be asleep
not notice them

she saw him the instant he ran out from the trees
racing toward her
more menacing than ever
braced herself for the inevitable attack

but the dog stopped suddenly
stood still
did not bark
looked questioningly at Maggie as she flew by

holding tight to the reins Maggie looked back
over her shoulder, astonished
to see the dog walk quietly back under the hedge

as if nobody had passed by

only then did Maggie hear
the silence
the stillness

Author's notes to the poem:
December 5, 1911. The Night That Amy.

This story was told to me often by my mother, Barbara Mackenzie Morse and her mother, Margaret (Maggie) Macaulay Mackenzie. Everything in this story was precious to me, particularly because it was about my grandmother whom I adored. As a child completely in tune with animals, it seemed real to me that a dog would just "know" the child had died as they passed by. I felt the dog was showing respect for Maggie and her daughter by curbing his aggressive behaviour.

In 1911 there were no lights anywhere, no street lights, indeed, no streets. Just cart tracks on a long road from the farms into the town of Oamaru.

The silence of the non-industrial society is difficult to imagine now. There were no telephones, no electricity, just farms and farmhouses in which most of the people were already asleep for the night.

The Southern Alps to the North behind her, the beautiful Waitaki River to the East of her, and surrounding her, only darkness. The way my grandmother Maggie described the landscape of her life at that time reminds me now of the silent loneliness of the land in novels by Dostoevsky or Tolstoy, or in the diaries of the Romanovs in exile, living deep in the Russian countryside.

I did not know the significance of this when I was a child, but Maggie was, in that year that her daughter Amy died, a young woman only 29 years old.

Marconi's Invention Does Not Amuse A Pre-Queen

I am intrigued by this woman
have admired her all my life
I listen to all the radio programs about her
following her death

endless true stories are told about her courage
her elegance, her sweetness during
all those one hundred and one years

including one not so sweet story
about her wedding in nineteen twenty three
a mere five years after great-uncle Geordie
returned from fighting in the great war
the war to end all wars

home to his farm on the
pastures of heaven near Awamoko
after sloshing for years through trenches
and months in hospital from the gas

his heart broken by the slaughter of young lads
his eyes imprinted forever with images of horses
helpless crying dying

he had sailed away from New Zealand in 1914
just a young man in his twenties
one of the first to risk his life for
King and Queen and Empire

he travelled to Europe
across the oceans his parents
traversed forty years before
when they left Scotland forever

an aide at the castle had suggested
Elizabeth's wedding ceremony
be recorded on the new wireless radio
so all could hear the young couple
plight their troth

she said no
that it would upset her
if her wedding ceremony were broadcast
she said:

"men wearing cloth caps might listen
might hear the ceremony in taverns
if such rough men were listening
it could tarnish the occasion"

she forbade the broadcast

kind and gentle Great-Uncle Geordie
wore a cloth cap
and when he returned from that
brutal, murderous, four year war
lifted many a pint at the Georgetown pub

Baling Wire, Fence Wire

when I was little my grandfather showed me
how to break wire by hand
fists clenched, he would hold the wire firmly
with only a few inches between each hand
then force the wire in opposite directions
at the point he had chosen

it was magic to me
my introduction to science
I could do this when I was four years old
and I can do it still
when it breaks, it intrigues me
to touch the broken ends
feel the heat created by friction

love and gratitude for him
flood my heart
every time

he called this a phenomenon
spoke the word with emphasis and care
on each of its syllables, separately
said it meant 'something that occurs'

I could tell he loved the word very much

years later, I learned what immensely strong
electrical forces are combined at a
molecular level when friction occurs

forces beyond imagining
like the unseen bonds
that can sustain the love of a child
for her grandfather across oceans
across continents
for more than fifty years

Penultimate

For Grandfather David Mackenzie

the second to last time ever I saw your face
you were in the Oamaru hospital
I was fifteen
we had just played the nurses' team
on the asphalt basketball court in the quadrangle
below your window
and won

I imagined you watching me
pleased as you always were with
every single thing I did
nodding at me, quietly saying
that's good Jack, that's good

before riding back to boarding school on a bike
owned by Miss Durham the home ec teacher
I went upstairs to see you
give you a hug, tell you we had won
imagine that, I said
our high school team
winning against the grown up nurses

you asked me to recite Masefield's "Sea Fever"
but very quietly please, you said
so as not to disturb the others in the ward and
when I stumbled on that line
'flung spray and blown spume'
we smiled together as we always did

when I finished the poem you said
that's good Jack, that's good

days later I could not cope with
the shocking news that you had died
I pretended it wasn't happening
took refuge in my dream world
until the day of the funeral

only when I saw you in your coffin
did I allow myself to
comprehend that you had died

I wanted to shriek and wail
sit hunched over beside you
keening in high notes
chanting a lament to assuage the
roaring pain
but that was not permitted
we were required to act with dignity
not make a public spectacle of ourselves

I had picked small blue flowers for you
put them in a jar no bigger than
an ink bottle
placed them beside the coffin

in that moment
I learned the awful meaning of the word
absence

Grand-dad Visits Canada

I dreamt about him last night
wearing his sou' wester and his
black lace up farm boots, the ones he
carefully greased with mutton fat
every night without fail
his ritual
to preserve the leather

I'm proud of you, he said
for making it on your own

but I didn't, I said
I was never alone
you told me that when I was
little, you said:
"I will never leave you"

at first I thought you meant
physically and I knew that was
not true because even at
seven years old
I knew that eventually
all organisms die
even if I didn't know the words

but you kept saying
"I will never leave you"
until I understood it which was
long after you were dead
when I found you right there
beside me
all through the hard times
cheering me on

Responsibility

in my recurring childhood dream
her slender legs
encased in silk stockings
her small feet in
expensive delicate shoes
ascended ornate metal stairs
which spiralled
high into a cloudless sky

I could see her feet far above me
climbing, climbing
and though I ran after her
leaping breathless
two steps at a time

I could not catch up to
hold her back

she kept climbing
her summer dress gently swirling
below her knees
as she placed one foot
then the other
deliberately on each step
relentlessly climbing
out of my reach

knowing
she would fall from the top
knowing
her painful cries would echo
down bleak canyons of my future
I kept trying night after night to
stop her
before she fell

Beggars Would Ride

my friend's mother just turned ninety
big shindig over at their house
five generations
the three year old wearing white organdy
her brother aged five
resplendent in a little boy suit
shiny shoes
to please great-great-grandmamma
born in a more formal time

it occurs to me with a fleeting stab of
sorrow that had my parents lived
they still would not be ninety

it's not fair

my parents died when I was twenty

I would like to attend such a party
march right in
see my father
give him hell
tell him a thing or two about his behaviour
the drinking
yelling obscenities at my perfect mother
curling the children's shell-like pink ears
into changed shapes
forever

but if he were still alive
we could have had forty years to sort this out so

perhaps I would just go over there
my grandchildren with me
big birthday cake in a box
my life's accomplishments in garlands around me like
strings of wildly brilliant coloured beads

sit beside his weary person
read to him

Swimming Against The Tide

took me all my life to understand
what went wrong with you

years of art therapy
painting brilliant oil colours in
thick textures on canvas
to deconstruct dissociative edifices
built by a child to protect herself from
your words
the words the words the words

thanks to counselling, I can now
embrace selective memories of you
admire your complex, creative genius
that invented and built
engineering systems
appreciate patent royalties that provided
music, art, private schools, and
the luxuries of our spacious brick house
with its leaf shaded tennis courts

I remember you at the wheel of your
white Terraplane sports car
taking Vanka our Russian Wolfhound for a run
along the road beside the ocean
her long hair rippling in the wind
as she raced to keep up with you

remember you with frost on your eyelashes
hiking on Franz Josef Glacier

remember those same eyelashes
soaked with tears of sorrow
when my mother threatened to leave you

your verbal abuse was a mystery to a child
directed only at my mother
not at your employees
never at your colleagues
who were all male
I was too young to understand you had been
programmed to assume power
over women

it makes no difference that it was not really you
that you were ill
your behaviour a blueprint of
your own private pain

I know it is true
but it does not provide solace

when I became strong enough to let the memories in
look at them through the clear light of healing
I could work my way through the echoes of terror
instilled by your violent words
but I could not change our history

I spent years of my life looking for you
trying to appease the alcohol rage-filled you
waiting for the other you to return

recognize me

I have no forgiveness for
your verbal abuse of my mother

what I do not yet understand is
the gratitude I feel

being able to call myself
your daughter

Seven Thousand Rivers

It Is Anna Whom We Mourn

Call The Name Gently: Ne-chaaaaa-ko

IT IS ANNA WHOM WE MOURN

Written in respectful memory of Anna Sorkomova, who took her own life in the winter of 1999 while attending University in Canada, far from her Siberian home. I wrote this poem/essay to honour her life, and to mourn her death.

What did I know of Siberia before I knew about Anna?

Stalin's gulags. Row upon row of barracks for dancers, artists, writers, dissidents, activists, innocents, thrust into new roles as slave labourers. The snow, the cold, the deprivation, the unimaginable distances between settlements where no roads existed. The exotic-sounding train: *Trans-Siberian Railway*. The very one which carried Tsar Nicholas and his family to house arrest and execution in Ekaterinburg/Sverdlovsk.

Fleeting summer images of plain, small, houses adorned with carved cornices, in bleak landscapes, beautiful flowers growing at their doorsteps. Stories of train travellers passing money out the open windows of passenger carriages to people who brought bread, vegetables and sunflower seeds to trains stopped near their villages.

Since Anna, I learned there is in Eastern Siberia a land called: Sakha, also called Yakutiya, land of diamonds, land of mineral riches, land of seven thousand rivers, land of the Yakut. The capital, Yakutsk, a city of about 250,000, lies north and east of Lensk, on the route of the mighty Lena River as it makes its 4,400 kilometre journey north to the Laptev Sea.

The central classroom building for International Programs of the new Yakutsk State University is a four story structure with six massive blue stone columns guarding its entrance. It overlooks a branch of the river, and is within walking distance of downtown.

Anna Sorkomova, 21, was a student at Yakutsk State University

It is here Anna studied, lived, laughed, and built her dreams.

The people of Sakha/Yakutiya possess a magnificent heritage which extends back to the Paleolithic Age. Anna's ancestors descended from tribes which migrated northward from Lake Baikal beginning in the tenth century A.D., mixing with the nomadic inhabitants of the area whose livelihood depended on gathering, fishing, hunting and reindeer herding. Russian settlers began moving into Sakha/Yakutiya in the early sixteen hundreds, and by 1630, the area came under Russian control. Even in the times of the rule of the Tsars, as well as during the Soviet Government which came to power after 1917, it was a place of exile for political prisoners.

Sakha/Yakutiya is rich in minerals and diamonds, as well as history. Due to the harsh terrain, road and rail transport is limited. Rivers and sled trails still serve as the most important transportation routes. The intention in Sakha/Yakutiya is to limit outside control of future industrial development to ensure the resulting wealth returns to the peoples of the area.

Two hours by small plane from Yakutsk, in a village called Sebyan Kyuyel, children were interviewed recently by a western journalist. These young students saw no contradiction in their expectations to maintain their ties to their traditional roots as reindeer herders, while studying at University to become multi-lingual teachers, doctors, lawyers, politicians, entrepreneurs, pilots and professors.

Anna Sorkomova, daughter of Sakha/Yakutiya, child of Eastern Siberia, spent the fall semester of 1999 in Canada, far from her beloved home.

At the University of Northern British Columbia, in Prince George, a city surrounded by forests, mountains, and wilderness, this young woman met her untimely and tragic death during the bitterly cold northern Canadian winter.

It is here that Anna died. Here.

I grieve for us
we who did not know of Anna's loneliness
her suffering
we who missed the opportunity to offer her
understanding, respect, help, and love.

Some of the cranes that fly home to Siberia from Bhutan in the springtime are thought to be over eighty years old. Stories about their flights over mountain ranges, rivers, lakes, and plains, over the vast taiga and tundra, speak of the wisdom the cranes carried back to the land of seven thousand rivers. Only when the cranes flew north over Sakha/Yakutiya did the long-maned, thick-haired, sturdy Yakut horse begin to shed its protective coat of winter hair. Then the people would say to one another: "Look, there are the cranes flying, the cranes are returning." Storytellers believed that the birds linked the souls of humans and animals together so that each could achieve compassion for the other by good deeds.

It is Anna whom we mourn

through the trees
your trees, Anna
there is a wailing sound:
the wind is sobbing with pain

the cranes are flying
carrying knowledge of sorrow,
carrying Canadian tears
our tears
we who learned
too late
how to care for Anna

Anna of the seven thousand rivers

Anna of the land of diamonds

Anna of the Lena

CALL THE NAME GENTLY: NE-CHAAAAA-KO

The people of the Cheslatta, hard-working, joyful, peaceful and self-sufficient, lived in an area of British Columbia that was flooded to meet the wants of a trans-national corporation. In 1952, families were torn from their traditional homeland solely for the purpose of enriching the already rich and powerful corporation. With no thought for the well-being, history, culture or future of those who had lived in these mountain valleys and plains for generations, corporate officials, aided by the Indian Agent of the Federal Government of Canada, contrived ways to effectively clear the land of people. They evicted them, then burned their houses. The workers employed to carry out these cruel acts refused to burn down the village church, but the Indian Agent hired a helicopter in Burns Lake and flew to the site to supervise the destruction, by fire, of a people's place of worship. Once the people were gone, the land that had supported them for generations disappeared under floodwaters as the corporation achieved its goal of changing the natural flow of the beautiful, wild, bountiful river: *The Nechako.*

My poem: *Call The Name Gently: Ne-chaaaaa-ko* was inspired by my reaction to viewing the film *"No Surrender,"* and by conversations with Chief Marvin Charlie of the Cheslatta Carrier Nation and Cheslatta Researcher Mike Robertson. Also, five years ago, I met a man who told stories about working in the Cheslatta area when he was seventeen years old, in the year 1923. He spoke of the area as if he were dreaming of a bountiful garden of Eden. He said: "I lived in Vancouver, so I had no idea of how beautiful the North could be. I came up there to make some money during the summer so I could go to school in the fall. It was the best summer of my life, and it was from the people of the Cheslatta that I learned how simple pursuits, close to the earth, could provide a good, satisfying life. I didn't hear what had been done to the river and those valleys until long after it was all a done deal, when I met someone at a farm sale in Kamloops and he said they had flooded it and sent the people packing. You know, when I heard what they had done to that beautiful land, those fertile valleys, and to the people and their way of life, it made me sick, it just made me sick."

Thinking about this man's memories of the summer of 1923 in those remote communities, in the context of the outrageous acts committed against the Cheslatta people by Government subsidized big-business interests, and reflecting on Margaret Gagnon's grandmother (Granny Seymour), and her statement about the need of a river to "flow on," gave birth to this poem.

My own certainty about the wisdom of animals, and the special deep knowing of those who live in the old ways, close to the earth, led me to reflect on the respect and honour that should be paid to sacred, ancient waters and homelands. Set against these beautiful images, it is clear to me that tampering with a river is an act of arrogance; an insult to the philosophy of living in harmony with the earth, a grievous and sorrowful wound inflicted against that which so freely and generously gives us life.

Tuatara is the Mäori word (*tua: dorsal, tara: spine)* for a nocturnal, lizard-like reptile, (*Sphaenodon Punctatum*) dark bronze- green with a row of yellow spines down its back, living on coastal islands near New Zealand. *Tuataras* are the last survivors of a whole group of ancient reptiles of the order *rhynchocephalia,* which flourished in the *Mezozoic* era.
(Webster's Encyclopaedic Unabridged Dictionary, New York, dilithium Press, 1989.)

Wildfire is a type of sheet lightning, without accompanying thunder, which lights up the sky and ocean at the horizon.

I think often about the vastness of the horizon of the Pacific Ocean. Did it light up with wildfire when my long ago maternal ancestors,

Catherine and Aulay Macaulay sailed across it in a tiny sailing barque called "*Invercargill*" in 1874? Did wildfire light the way of the ship "*Blenheim*" carrying my paternal great-great grandparents across the ocean from Scotland to New Zealand, arriving on Christmas Day, 1840?

Two sides of my personal world, maternal and paternal ancestors, suffered the effects of the Scottish Highland Clearances. Their houses had been burned down, their livelihoods destroyed, their lands confiscated, to make way for the indulgences of the rich.

More than a century apart, these two crimes against people and their land, the Highland Clearances and the flooding of the Cheslatta land, were set in motion by an identical motive: greed of the already rich. I despair of the behaviour of the powerful of this world, their obliviousness to their own privilege, their sublime indifference toward ordinary people.

In looking for solace from the terrible knowledge of what can result from this indifference, I find comfort and hope in images of mountains, rivers, animals, and the constancy suggested by such wonders as the timeless generations of the *Tuataras* of Knights' Islands.

Call The Name Gently: Ne-chaaaaa-ko

Margaret Gagnon, an aboriginal elder
told us a story her grandmother told her
about rivers:
"a river doesn't turn back on itself
it flows on
knowing the danger of re-visiting
old hurts"

Tuataras know this
older than dinosaurs
they are still alive on the Knights' Islands
in the South Pacific Ocean

their giant eyes can see for centuries

in 1952
without consulting Margaret's grandmother
or the river
the guys from Alcan drilled a hole
in a mountain
so they could turn water
from a sacred river
back on itself

now they are at it again
they who don't know
sacred
from a hole in the ground

first, let us dance a path to the river
sing water songs
ask forgiveness for old hurts
of the nineteen fifties

the Tuataras have been consulted
on pacific winds
through an indigo sky
they send

wildfire

to light our way

Courage Of The Wild Crocus

Courage Of The Wild Crocus

Deep In The Heart Of Stockholm

May I Introduce Anne-Marie Edward

No Visible Signs

Domestic Peace

True Tellings

Linda Who Runs With The Flowers

Come Home

Courage Of The Wild Crocus

in Manitoba
there's a crocus called
ears-of-the-earth

this harbinger of springtime
messenger from underground
sends up tentative green leaves
to test the air for
nurturing warmth
so flowers can venture into growth

like the sensitive, tender ears of
small, vulnerable children
these little flowers in their bright colours
need early protection from storms
so they can burst forth into their lives
take possession of themselves
flourish in all their glory

Deep In The Heart Of Stockholm

she has been married to him thirty years

when I call her
she always asks me to call back later when
he
is not there so she can
really talk
because when he is there she cannot,
you know, talk

I go to their house to visit her
my lifelong friend
travelling five hundred miles to see her

within minutes of my arrival he yells at her
calls her stupid, which she is not
then he stomps out of the room

in the sunlight of their yellow kitchen I can see
fragments of her soul
flying around the room
trying to connect again with one another

my God, I say
where does all the love go?

she turns on me
tells me it is all my fault
that if I would just keep quiet
stop saying things such as

where does all the love go?

she wouldn't be unhappy with him at all

it is only my words
mine
that make her feel so awful

May I Introduce: Anne-Marie Edward

I wrote this poem to try to understand and record the immense depth of the tragedy of December 6, 1989. By learning some of the details of just one of the women's lives, I want this poem to honour and respect the complexity of the loss of all the Montreal Massacre women, and all murdered and missing women, to show how much human richness has been taken from the world, and to mourn and grieve their loss. Anne-Marie's story was obtained from her mother, Suzanne LaPlante Edward of Montreal, who gave me permission to write this poem and publish it in memory of her daughter. Suzanne has worked tirelessly since the events, campaigning for gun control in Canada. This poem is read at memorial services in British Columbia every year on the anniversary of the massacre. **We will never forget, never.**

Part One

in her kayak classes
she had difficulty mastering the roll
easy to do in the swimming pool
difficult in the running river
she kept trying

it is necessary to learn the roll in case the
kayak capsizes, it is this skill that turns
kayak, kayaker and paddle
right side up, unharmed

out one day with her group on the river
practising, she tried the roll and disappeared
the current took her quickly downstream
upside down, underwater

her companions followed her course
searched for her, found her a long way down
completely soaked but laughing, jubilant
hey! she shouted, waving her paddle wildly
I guess I finally mastered that roll eh?

her nickname was "Spunky"
a woman who applied herself diligently
to everything:

English, French, Spanish, German
a student who excelled in all her classes
played classical guitar, climbed mountains
earned herself a place on an expert ski team
a woman who took time to volunteer
helping children in need

Part Two

I want to forget the name of the person who
killed fourteen women including
Anne-Marie Edward with a gun
his name doesn't matter, their names do

I heard the news out at my rural mailbox
from my seventy year old neighbour
a quiet, dignified soldier from the
second world war

I had been hoping for a letter from my son
travelling in New Zealand, or from my
daughter, studying at Simon Fraser University
thinking about my children as we do
always, always thinking about our children

my neighbour drove up in his old truck
opened the door on the driver's side
swung his body around
put his feet in their winter boots
down on the snowy ground
his hands on his knees

tears poured down his lined face
he said: somebody has shot fourteen women
in Montreal,
women, he said, shaking his head, crying
all of them women
what, he said, have we come to?

Part Three

unbelievable then, it seems worse now
I am desperately sad, furiously angry
that we live in a world where there is
a war against women's bodies
their being

Anne-Marie Edward:

loving parents, a family
a remarkable, unique woman with a
delightful sense of humour
many accomplishments
a promising future

lost because she was a woman
murdered for no reason other than
being a woman
living in a society with blinders on
a society in denial

Anne-Marie Edward

multiply by fourteen

and then again,
and again,
and again…..

No Visible Signs

hadn't watched Startrek for years till tonight
waiting in the bank lineup at the mall
where they provide a television set so
clients won't notice
the average wait is fourteen point four minutes

the Captain is time travelling
also trying something new
lifestyle travelling
right into someone else's life

one minute he is the Captain
a high profile guy
next minute he is an aged man
sitting in a rocking chair, wrinkled, raging,
thrashing about in indignation
very pissed off

"this is not my life" he shouts
but nobody can hear him

what if it were possible to
walk a mile in another's shoes
wake up one morning
grateful not to have metamorphosed into
a spider overnight
only to find Robespierre
staring back from the bathroom mirror
or worse, Rasputin
yawning, bleary eyed
with no intention of shaving off that beard

imagine waking up as Imelda of the shoes
conducting her famous anti-poverty campaign
from her two thousand dollar a day hotel suite

my life suddenly becomes more valuable to me
as I think of dozens of people I would not want to be

especially Mari Simpson
lived in Prince Rupert when she was a kid
coming home from school one day a man
jumped out of the bushes
grabbed her, overpowered her

carried her back into the trees
she was eleven at the time
didn't tell anyone about it
until she was twenty three

that day, she said, that day I got
raped
I walked on home afterwards
when I got there my aunt said to me

how was your day?

I said fine, it was fine

Domestic Peace

the instant he hit my son's precious
head, banging it on the wooden floor
I knew I had stayed way too long
trying to keep promises I made
in a church on my wedding day

during the night after a
terrible, horrific scene that now
thirty three years later
doesn't bear thinking about
I fled with the children

all I had to my name was
fifty bucks in cash
a signed i.o.u. for a horse I had sold for
one hundred dollars
an ancient powder blue VW bug
four hand made feather quilts
the children's clothes
a few of their toys and books

and, in case we got hungry

twelve large jars
of home canned sliced peaches

True Tellings

I am a big fan of my friend Jocelyn
she is wise and kind, hilariously funny
mother of two and madly, wildly
passionately in love with her husband

but sometimes memories of her past
return to haunt her

this morning as we stand talking in the
bright sunshine Jocelyn tells me that
when she was young, her mother's
husband used to beat her

stunned, I ask her: how bad? as if there is
a degree of being beaten up above which is
graded bad, and below, well: not so bad

her navy blue eyes fill with ancient pain:
you know, the usual stuff, hands around my
neck throttling me, shoving me, beating my
head against the bathroom wall
you know the kind of stuff they do

my reaction is pure fury
I am filled with a flood of vindictive
anger toward him

rage turns to tears
waves of sadness assail me as I think about her
powerlessness when she was only fourteen

tears run in rivers down my face, and she
my kind Jocelyn, gently reaches out and touches
my arm
says: I shouldn't have told you
I didn't mean to upset you

Linda Who Runs With The Flowers

early spring
the Nechako pours itself into the Fraser
at Cottonwood Park

the Fraser, deeper and wider
accepts the dancing waters of the Nechako
like a mother horse nuzzling a frisky colt

we are gathered for a silent vigil
ceremony of the flowers
honouring women who have suffered violence
at the hands of men

women of all ages, cultures
in jeans and ball caps, saris and babushkas
come from home, from work, from farms
another just minutes off a plane from Montréal
wearing designer shoes
there are children, supportive men
bicycles, dogs on leashes

roses and carnations are kept cool in a
galvanized washtub
someone has brought a huge urn of coffee
there are no speeches

at exactly one o'clock
people start taking flowers to the river
no one speaks
the only sound is that of the water

for the time it takes to throw a flower on the
flowing current
each is alone with her own particular memory
some women fight back tears
thinking of their mothers, grandmothers, daughters, friends
themselves

the flowers float downstream in silent tribute
we stand
watching them go

we are less than fifty metres from the confluence of
two majestic rivers
watching a carpet of flowers
floating testimony to centuries of pain
borne by women
abused by men who are often
their partners

I see Linda from Scotland climbing along the rocky shore
down a path by the water
she is running downstream
running beside the flowers
accompanying them
grown woman with the heart of a child
leaping over rocks and stones
over logs lying on the bank
through long grass and scrub willows
communing with the flowers
guarding them till they reach the big water where
the Fraser will carry them to the ocean

her long celtic hair has curled up in the
dampness of the mist from the water
I watch her run
fleet of Scottish Canadian foot
her hair blowing out bonny behind her

she is running for us all
she is running for me

that me of thirty years ago
too busy shielding my children from harm to
comprehend the horror of hearing him say
oh, it's you?
did you know I thought I had killed you?
I went to the doctor after you left with the children
and I said to him: hey Doc, lissen up
I have killed my wife and children and what is
really funny
is that I can't remember where I put the bodies
ha ha ha, imagine that, I couldn't find your bodies
isn't that funny?
ha ha ha

Come Home

in a moonlit room
a cast iron bathtub with clawed feet
on a hardwood plank floor

yellow freesias in a
cobalt glass

ribbons to bind your hair

hot water and silence

thick thirsty towels
to drink up your pain

Twelve Salmon Pink Roses

Why I Went Back To School

Slipstream

Greedspeak

We Forgot To Keep Our Ear To The
    Ground

Where Have You Gone, Crosby Stills
    Nash and Young

Watch The Wall My Darlings

Yet Another G8 Conference, Ho Hum

Academic Language As A Refuge In A
    Disintegrating World

Yak Flatterers

Deliveries

Collateral Damage

Sunday Morning Downtown Haiku

In Praise Of Good Men

Why I Went Back To School

is it true that Marco Polo was there when the burial
party returned from the funeral of Kublai Khan?
what relation was Genghis to Kublai? was he perhaps
his grandfather? Did Kublai live in
Peking? Do the words Genghis Khan mean
ruler of all the oceans? was Genghis's mother a
single parent living in poverty?

the texts say that all two thousand members of the
burial party were killed by an army of four
hundred men who rode out to meet them, then
killed them, then cut an ear from each so that
all would be accounted for

when the four hundred returned, ears in sacks
is it true that they were also killed? if so, how does
anyone know this story? was Marco Polo spying
on the whole operation? did he write of it?
if so, did he stick to the facts? in other words
did he tell the truth

it is written that Genghis Khan said: *there is no
greater joy in life than sweeping your enemies
before you, in terror, then capturing them
killing them, raiding their camp, looting their
treasures, raping their wives and daughters*

no greater joy

no greater joy?

how long will I have to stay in University
before I understand this

Slipstream

deep snow outside
she comes to my house with twelve
salmon pink roses

we celebrate with tea
conversation

"I worry about these roses"
she says

"they are grown in Chile"

she pronounces this
Cheee-lay

thirty years since Allende
the soccer stadium
the guitarist's hands cut off
at his wrists

roses to Canada
in silver planes ·

vapour trails like thorns
scratch a sky

innocent

full of melodies

Greed Speak

sitting here with a few ancient ancestors
drinking tea, reading the papers
talking

we easily inhabit the same place
same time

these historical sweet creatures from other decades
other centuries
accompany me through difficult terrain
like guardian outriders on
dangerous journeys

our memories are long
we do not believe that history is gone
it is here with us
pouring the tea

pervasive use of a strange new language
devoid of meaning
distresses us
we wonder if we have gone mad
without noticing the transition

newspapers use different meanings for old words
as if someone has been quietly working
behind the scenes
Cratchit-like in a green visored eye-shield
meticulously entering a large ledger with
new meanings for words that once described
things that make life precious

air, water, morning dew, suppertime, land, integrity

obliterating old meanings
inserting those that meet this criterion:
the new meaning must serve only one master: profit

which Scrooges employ such a lexicographer?
global criminals? global business?
both act triumphant as if they have a secret up their
collective arrogant sleeve

my ancestors and I contemplate the word: *harvest*

revered word
shimmering gold, redolent with images of
stooked sheaves
fragrant and warm in the setting sun

we weep for the word harvest
so recently betrayed
stolen by seed pirates and foresters
distorted now to mean:

"it's mine"

my companions prepare to leave
drain their teacups
fold the papers
saddened by knowing this
take-over of language
is a catastrophe that
endangers us
causes us to lose memory

they know
all is not safely gathered in

and the winter storms have
already begun

We Forgot To Keep Our Ear To The Ground

after Culloden
everything went to hell
for a hundred years or more

the big boys
seduced by the siren song of money
didn't want anything untidy such as
people
cluttering up their lucrative grazing runs

so they burned them out of their houses
cleared them out of the glens
chased them away to the coasts
to eke out a living there
or emigrate to New Zealand
Australia, Canada

sold out of their birthright
by the chieftains of their own clans

now it's happening here
our elected chieftains selling us out
to the money-junkies
who bought up our governments
when we weren't looking

same old story

they burn
we flee

where do we go this time

Where Have You Gone, Crosby Stills Nash and Young

the radio alarm wakes me up at five thirty
Neil Young is singing four dead in
oh-hi-oh
thirty three years since it happened
seems like yesterday until I remember my
daughter, the lean laughing kayaker
is now thirty four

when she was a one year old baby
the murders at Kent State
made me wonder how I dared
to have the arrogance to bring children
into this terrible world where the
powerful solve their problems with guns
if we don't stand to attention when they speak

the news is on
there is a protest on the highway between
Williams Lake and Quesnel
to draw attention to the fact that the new
sweep-everything-clean-for-the-rich Provincial
government wants to close down the Marguerite Ferry
which has carried people from
one side of the Fraser River to the other
for generations

a protester interviewed by CBC's reporter says:

"The reason they are closing it down you know is because
it's mainly aboriginal and rural people who use this ferry.
They wouldn't remove the ferry if it were carrying their cronies
from lunch to the golf course."

Watch The Wall My Darlings

it is a dance we do
when he isn't looking
we creep around behind him
climb invisible on his shoulders
so we can peer through his eyes
at the world, at ourselves
see what he sees
divine who it is that he wants us
to be
what it is that he wants us
to say

once we know what he wants
we can become it
please him
say the right things
prevent him from being
angry

like ancient funeral horses
hooves muffled on
cobblestones
we do all of our walking in

silent shoes

My inspiration for the title "Watch The Wall My Darlings" is from the chorus of Rudyard Kipling's "The Smuggler's Song" (in "Hal o' the Draft", Chapter VIII of his book "Puck Of Pook's Hill", published in 1906.) There was a conspiracy of silence to protect the powerful that accompanied the violence of the criminals who smuggled contraband goods. Sometimes those who were looking the other way were often the beneficiaries of the smuggled goods. Even if they were not, it was dangerous to acknowledge that one had observed any smuggling activity, as the penalty could be death.

The connection between the survival strategy behaviour of victims of domestic abuse and victims of repressive political regimes interests me because similarities exist in the damage inflicted on the personality. We learn to see ourselves, our world, and our needs through eyes other than our own. This can lead to imprisonment of the mind, and consequent loss of our own identity.

Yet Another G-8 Conference, Ho Hum.

what does the G-8 have to do with me?
who are these guys?
what are they discussing?
from whose perspective?
do they know what they are talking about?

what interest do they show in the life of my family in
particular my baby grand-daughter who will
inherit the world they create?

why don't they do something about poverty
disarmament, pollution, and violence
while they are at it they might also tackle
patronage and nepotism

if these are the 'fathers' of the greatest nations
in the whole wide world
why aren't they concerned that powerful forces
are at work lobbying governments to
disregard human needs
so there will be
more and more and more and more and more
profits for the rich?

on the news I see images of these men
whisked across the world in private jets
to attend closed meetings in
luxurious palaces, villas, mansions
in surroundings of great beauty
and rarefied air

if these men are so important
why do they and their activities change
nothing in my life for the better?

Academic Language As A Refuge In A Disintegrating World

to understand language
it is necessary to learn that
hetero-glossia means:
a multiplicity of voices that are
inter-related dialogically in a text

to understand ideology
we need to know that the word
hegemony refers not only to leadership
and influence but to
undue influence

to understand patriarchy
it is helpful to look at the fact that
most religious organizations are
controlled by men whose emphasis on
the sanctity of the monogamous family
stands as a model for society and
that in state patriarchy
a woman is considered subordinate to the state

it is assumed that men have a collective right
indistinguishable from the state which means:
power belongs to males

power dominates, enters every aspect of our lives
every activity
power is a social and psychological phenomenon
it can control our thoughts, form our feelings

to resist, it is wise to acquire language
with which to define the problem

Yak Flatterers

Published in
the Federation of B.C. Writers Anthology, 2003.

the professor had lived in Tibet
spoke eight languages
was teaching us latin declensions

we were off in teenage dreams
rock and roll, boys, beach parties

we tried to get him talking about travel
divert him from grammar
he would become excited
speak two or three languages at once
without noticing

someone asked him
what future can there be for this country
now occupied by China?

"Ach" he said "very triste"

he told us that in the Himalayas
it is necessary to sing to the yak
appease him
before loading him with all your freight

you hum words
tell him how enchanting he is
how beautiful
in a low voice you describe rhododendrons
blooming in thousands of different shades
in Tibet

your yak-seducing tone
lulls him into complacency
allowing you to creep up on him
invade his life
placate him sufficiently to get

your load
on
his back

Deliveries

twenty two years old, new in town, new job
assistant to the finance company skip tracer
recording his telephoned conversations
while he harasses clients: pay up or else

he called an elderly woman who said:
I cannot pay you
my husband has just died
it was he who incurred this debt
I have no money
my daughter is sick
we have to pay for his funeral

the skip tracer whose name I no longer recall but
whose facial expressions I will never forget says:
these are not our problems
we will send someone to pick up your television set
this afternoon

I turn off the tape recorder and
in my immigrant ignorance
say to him as he hangs up:
this is unfair
the woman's husband has just died
can't you give her some time?

his pointed features turn meaner than I thought possible
he tells me I have not been hired to give my opinions
but to do what he asks
you are a typist, he says
just do what you are told

I break my own record that day
start a new job at eight thirty in the morning
get fired before ten a.m. coffee break

Collateral Damage: Father Of All Euphemisms

the term collateral damage relates to lateral but not to literal, it is
something to ignore, perceived to be an inevitable, subordinate, minor
disadvantage of a process whether that be war, new colonies, or total
absolute power over all living things: a delusion of immaculate
grandeur, a paranoia of power: a *powernoia*

those directing the carnage assure us the damage is regrettable but
necessary and also justified because of the nobility of their purpose and
the fact that God, who must be a very busy boy, is on their side

well what about soldiers going totally bonkers sixty years after the first
world war driven mad by elderly nightmares about men they knew
intimately as youths having their heads blown off and men screaming
lying dying in mud after being shelled and losing all four of their
limbs, did they count that in their bloody ghastly trench warfare
calculations, no they didn't and how about General Douglas Haig
whose philosophy about the soldiers who fought in World War One
was that really, they were fighting not only with God on their side,
God at that time being a tall thin bearded white guy in the sky, but
with a chance of going to a Christian Paradise if they died in battle; its
true, look it up, isn't that a big surprise, the Paradise promise, where
have I heard that before and very recently too

and the damage of verbal abuse if I may be so bold as to mention it
which is rife in family violence as well as in legislatures where people
of power consider that they can say whatever they want no matter how
untrue or harmful it is to those who may, by accident, have elected
them and it won't take sixty years maybe only five or ten for the
powerful whose verbal abuse is polished, manipulative and delivered
with a chilling smile to put paid to the middle class now they have
completely done in the poor

another sixty years later, a totally different set of sixty years, generations later, one small child will be a family matriarch with wonderful children and grandchildren and time and opportunity to put her feet up and have a cup of tea or study or whatever she wants when suddenly, out of a clear blue sky, she finds herself having flashbacks and nightmares as the verbal abuse she heard as a child comes back to terrorize her mind so that instead of joining her friends in a game of tennis down at the senior's centre, she has to stay home and calm herself so she doesn't go running insanely down the street screaming for help for her mother begging someone, please, to rescue her Mummy whose fearful wailing she hears in a mind awash with tears she didn't have time or permission to cry until now

Sunday Morning Downtown Haiku

driving to the writing workshop
I pass some children
dressed up working children

I don't want to accept the existence of
abuse as if it were acceptable simply
because of its existence
covered up by
mindless clichés, aphorisms such as

oh well its always been there
the oldest profession you know

they are children for godsake
they should be home, safe
not forced into the vile global
commerce of the sex trade

I hate those stealers of souls
one lone male driver in
each fancy car driving by real slow
checking out the kids for sale

our first warm-up writing exercise
at the Sunday morning workshop
is to write one haiku, any topic
five syllables, seven syllables
then five syllables

I wrote this
called it *"Solipsism"*

silver haired daddies
cruise early morning mean streets
seek receptacles

In Praise Of Good Men

we had many uncles and great-uncles
as well as the younger uncles
married to my aunties
the Mackenzie girls from Georgetown

the uncles respected women
were kind to children and animals
made jokes, played fiddles, danced jigs
told stories, picked berries, made jam
carved wooden whistles, made rope slippers
loved their vegetable gardens, their chickens
ran their own businesses and farms
went away to wars, came back, went fishing
rode and raced horses, cared for their elders
became very stern if we did something wrong
kept an eye on us, encouraged us to study
they knew all of the words to all of the songs
and they taught them to us
we were connected to them through
laughter, joy, and mutual respect
the uncles made being good men look easy

now with two fine grown sons of my own I see
it can be difficult to be a good man
in a world where social influences
encourage men to become the opposite

I have learned what an achievement it is
to be a good man

I think there should be more appreciation
to honour those men we all know
of whom it can be said, loudly and clearly:

he is one good man, that one

Chaos And Delight: The Melody Of What Happens

Shedding Naïve Illusions At Last

The Gift

Lament For The Rose

Running Over Hub

Twenty Two Below With The Wind
    Chill

Anna The Magnificent

On With The New

Bart And Brenda

Indelible

Ectopic Pregnancy

Close To The Surface

Gladys

Is Anyone There?

Getting To Know Great-Aunt Delia

The Speed Of Loneliness

Must Be True, It Was In The
    Newspaper

Legacy

Shedding Naïve Illusions at Last

we are like the flounder

while both eyes on one side scan
justice, honour and truth

absorb light from a path seen as
integrity

life continues on the shadow side where
we cannot see
and would not believe it
if we could

The Gift

in Banff
deer came to our cabin door like
kittens
waiting to be fed

early some mornings I would go with him
my husband
this symphony violinist turned truckdriver
in his five ton oil truck
up the Banff-Jasper highway
my skis tied to the back platform
beside the forty five gallon oil drums

he would drop me off at Peyto Peak
to hike in to the snowline

he was pleased I was doing
exactly what I wanted, skiing
completely alone
climbing up, skiing down
climbing up, skiing down
on an isolated mountainside
while he drove up to the Columbia Icefields
and Jasper
delivered his loads of fuel
picked me up on the way back

we would drive home to Banff by starlight
singing

one day they wanted all the fuel at the Icefields
no need to go on up to Jasper
he arrived back at Peyto hours early
walked in to where I was skiing

we ate our lunch
he said he would hike up over the peak
to the south side
see what he could see
rather than watch me climb up, ski down
climb up, ski down

I was taking off my skis when he returned
running toward me, smiling
telling me he had found a paradise over the ridge
miles and miles of
yellow red purple blue orange flowers
fields of them
stretching forever
on the south-facing slope

he held out his hands
they were full of flowers
for me

short thick-stemmed stubby alpine wildflowers
a palette bouquet picked one by one
while he waited for me to finish
climbing up, skiing down
climbing up, skiing down
that spring
in the Canadian Rockies

this is what it was like
before

I do not know the exact moment it changed
it was imperceptible

I tumbled down into an abyss with him
a millimetre at a time

by the time I became aware of the falling
by the time it became a nightmare

I had completely forgotten what it felt like
to hold

rocky mountain wildflowers

Lament For The Rose

slowly, his secret descent
into the heart of that compelling addiction

stole from me
my treasured companion

when I realized there was
nobody on this earth
who could take his place
I lost my ability to fly
in dreams

my feathered arms albatross wide
soaring over oceans
coral reefs
remote mountain passes

over whole countries full of hedged fields
painted houses beside rivers
my soul aloft

my heart beating crimson with joy

Author's note:

William Blake's poem "The Sick Rose" (The Essential Blake, 1987,
Ecco Press) inspired me to write about the effects of the loss of a
beloved soulmate through addiction:

(O rose thou art sick/The invisible worm
That flies in the night/In the howling storm

Has found out thy bed/Of crimson joy.
And his dark secret love/Does thy life destroy.)

Running Over Hub

by mistake she said
she ran over him by mistake last summer
astonished when she saw
his bruised body
lying on the cement of the
hotel parking lot

"talk to me"
she screamed to the lifeless body
"please"

emotional but composed in court
she told how desperately hard she had
worked to save her marriage
even quitting her job
to give them more time to
make love three times a night and
she promised hub she would have surgery
to make her breasts bigger then
spent hours cooking his favourite meals but
nothing worked

running over him had been an accident
a mistake made
after she found him in *flagrante delicto*
at a hotel room with his new lover

recalling the confrontation that followed
she agrees she was distraught
the night she physically assaulted hub's lover
before returning to her car in the parking lot
but she has no idea how he ended up under
the wheels

she cannot answer the question, no
she does not remember what she was thinking at the time

nothing, she replies, nothing

I wasn't thinking anything

Twenty Two Below With The Wind Chill

pulling on my toque against the
fierce cold
I see him striding up Third Avenue
reflected in the windows of Black's Furs
green parka, lumberjack shirt
thick graying beard
battered cowboy hat

the wind makes my eyes water
clouds my vision
but I'm sure it's him
my old dear friend, so I follow
wanting to say hello, ask him
does he know he appears in some of my
poems as the good man he was

I walk into Canada Trust
he is at the teller
suddenly I am not sure

this man looks sturdier
not so thin and the face that
turns toward me is blank

what was I thinking?

following strange men around
at ten in the morning on a bitterly cold day

I forgot the years that have passed
forgot that he no longer lives here
and that he was gone from my life
long before he moved away

Anna The Magnificent

is going to Turkey for a month by herself
to explore remote villages
travel old roads, visit mosques

someone asked her if she was afraid
going all alone to such an exotic place

afraid?
no, she said I learned very young not to
waste life being afraid watching my
Aunty Mary
scared of this and scared of that worried
about Uncle Irwin
who was what they used to call *poorly*
she was afraid he would take ill and die leaving her
all alone not even in Turkey but
right here in Canada alone with his
pension plan if you please
now look at him Uncle Irwin is a widower
Aunty Mary died at fifty worried herself to death
he is having a great old time on his little farm
killing pigs gathering eggs going around his greenhouse
every morning singing to his tomato plants doing
what he calls his fertilizing which is actually
pollinating with a tiny paintbrush
blossom to blossom

he is seventy three years old
grows the best tomatoes in the district
dances every dance Saturday nights at the
Legion Hall where all the women are after him because
he is a lot of fun and a great dancer but he isn't
interested and he doesn't want anyone

worrying about him ever again

no, I am not afraid of going to Turkey
all by myself

not at all

On With The New

I adored him
she said
perhaps I should say
I adored what I thought was him
but it was a spare persona he
was using when we met
and for a few years after that

we married
had children together
I watched as
the person I loved
gradually became somebody else
his behaviour toward me and the children
was inexplicable
finally broke my heart

I kept waiting
for the person I had known to return
but he couldn't
he didn't have that program anymore

the saddest loss was in learning
it was the spare
the mythic persona
who had known
and loved
me

Bart And Brenda

twenty years ago she was a single parent
living in Prince George
playing tennis, cross country skiing
trying to get a career going that would
support her in the future

two of her friends started up a new business
a dating service
asked her if she would be a sort of
trial client
a freebee on whom they could practise their service

there was this, well, difficult client
he might turn out to be what they called
hard to place
would she help them?

not for dating thanks
I will have cups of coffee and chats and maybe, just maybe
a movie but I will pay my own way and I will not date
the thought of dating gives me the shivers
I'll help you out seeing its your new business
and let you know what I think but dating?
no way

so they fix her up with this guy called Bart
coffee only
he describes himself as a teacher, a
professional who moves socially, he says,
only with the rich
the influential

well!
bore the you-know-whats off a brass monkey so
she told them she didn't want to see
him again, ever
she was no longer interested in being a trial client either
not for the sake of their friendship
not even to help them get their business off the ground

count me out, she said

when Bart called she said
no, I am not interested in seeing you again
no, not even for coffee

three years later, on the grapevine, she hears that
he talks about her
as if
they used to go out

seven years after that she meets him one day in a bank
he greets her like a long lost lover
eyes narrowing as he says, smiling
we had good times, didn't we?

My God, thinks Brenda
this man must have me confused with someone else
or have I confused him with someone else?
or did I miss something?
he says to her:
could we get back together again?

she looks sternly at him and says no
we never were together Bart
really, we were not
I assure you

yesterday
twenty years since she first refused to see him
she runs into him in the deli
he is with a charming woman who wears a wedding ring
and he is no longer bald
did I mention bald?

Brenda had always wondered if stories about
bald men being sexier than other men were true
ever since she saw Yul Brynner in *The King And I* and
just last week
an attractive bald man had walked into her office
wearing a T shirt that said:

this is not a bald patch
it is a solar panel
for a sex machine

Bart though, now sports a red
yes, red
carrot top toupee
which does not sit well with his
heavy black eyebrows

reeling from this apparition, she says hello

he introduces the two women and tells his wife:
this is Brenda
we used to go out, years ago

Brenda is amazed
will this never end?

she ponders her current life
her husband of the past eighteen years
her fluffed out matronly feathers under which
nine grandchildren now spread their tiny wings
she thinks of all these people who inhabit her life
all of the years and changes since 1980
she thinks about her own ageing, her ailments
the long years it has been since she picked up
a tennis racquet

she looks at Bart's unlined, bland face as he
grins at her leeringly
never mind the fact that is wife is standing
right beside him

for some odd reason
she hears this voice
which happens to be hers
ringing out over the salads, the pastrami, the bratwurst

now Bart:

have you been running around on me?

Indelible

forty years later she wakes up screaming
dreaming a night when she was nine
he picked up a heavy oak chair
raised it behind his head
smashed it down on the long dining room table
while his children, his wife
ran out of the way

crystal glasses, Belle Fiore plates, chips of wood
flying in pieces

red wine staining white linen

her husband reaches both his arms around her
hush hush, it is alright, you had a bad dream
you are safe here with me

crying, broken, disoriented
her eyes search her husband's face
wild in her need for refuge

mummy! she demands of a woman dead for thirty years
if you had known this could last for so long
would you have left him?
no matter how hard, how poor?

her husband lovingly strokes her arm, her hair
puts a soft pillow behind her rigid shoulders

yes, he says, yes of course she would have
had she known, she would have fled with you
braved all the consequences
but it was the times
the rules, the shame, the stigma of divorce
laid at the feet of women
she did her best with what she knew

she just did not know
what it would do
to you

Ectopic Pregnancy
(Greek: "Ektopos": out of place)

my son and his partner wanted this baby
a planned joyfully anticipated event
until today, three o'clock

I walk out of hospital doors to a parking lot
which slopes away on both sides
as if it were part of a concrete planet
in miniature
a planet of loneliness, illness, heartache, loss

the sky is dull with grey clouds through which I hear
keening lament, generations old, from across the world
and I start to weep for my mother, her mother
all of us

I who have always been a strong woman
a rower of boats
ferrying people to safety in storms
passionate in my conviction that
a woman's choice is hers alone to make
find myself devastated by the term: ectopic
a word that leaves a woman no choice

Close To The Surface

Beverley is making home-made pizza for her daughter
and some friends thinking about her own life at that
age, well they can't possibly understand what it was
like there was no pill, no such thing as a support
group, no honesty, and then of course the church
it was difficult to admit you even liked sex
in case somebody thought you were a slut and when she
got pregnant, her parents sent her away to
one of those places where they adopt out the baby
and you pretend forever that it never happened

in the other room they are talking about guys
safe sex, somebody's sudden passion for a new
student over at the college

she listens to them talk and laugh, comfortable with
themselves, envies them their freedom

she dusts the pizza dough with flour, rolls it out
puts on the toppings ready for the oven
can you hear us Mum? yes, every word
I can't see you, but I sure can hear you
they all laugh, one says: your Mum is so cool

she thinks this oven is what is too cool it needs
turning up to four hundred and suddenly a wave
of disbelief hits her as she thinks of the child she
gave up thirty years before, how important
it was then to keep it a secret and how it doesn't
matter now but its too late and how she is always
looking into every pair of blue eyes
wondering is she still here in Montreal, what
happened to her, wondering is she a movie star,
a singer, a doctor, somebody's wife, somebody's mother
maybe a druggie, maybe a nun

is the pizza ready yet Mum?

I don't know I don't know I don't know I don't know

Gladys

Gladys
who lives away out in the bush
miles from Prince George
hangs out her one scott paper towel to dry

she grew up in the thirties depression
can't get over the cutting down of trees
to make paper towels

she only has a grade three education
after that she had to stay home
milk cows
help out with food for the family

but she has the same philosophy as
Winston Churchill
Prime Minister of Great Britain
who said, in 1929
while visiting Canada

"imagine them cutting down all these
lovely trees
and calling it

civilization"

Is Anyone There?

she is far away, alone
in a land full of darkness and pain

enduring shrieking flashes of light
behind her closed lids
sadness seeping like lead
dogged, relentless
through to the centre of her bones

at the same time
she works
performs her duties
collects her paycheque
meets friends
goes to the library
eats dinner
as if she were a real person

he has made love to somebody else

in some languages there is no verb
to be

she used to wonder what that signified
to live without knowledge of
I am/you are/she is/they are

now that she knows

she wishes that
she did not

Getting To Know Great-Aunt Delia

as a young woman she worked her way through the
great depression at five dollars a month
doing housekeeping and something known as
light farm work
seven days a week
twelve hours a day

she describes this period in her life as
university of the soil

well into her sixties when I first met her
she drove up our farm road in her son's
mint condition sixty three Chev Malibu
bright red
dual chrome exhausts

here I am she said
like it or not
time we got acquainted

I had built myself a little woven willow fence that
fanned out from both sides of the duckhouse door
forming an open-ended enclosure
a structure designed to make duck-securing orderly
a miniature buffalo jump
to guide my fifty Muscovy ducks in at night

but they moved in waves like sheep
one would miss the willow fence
turn the opposite way
encouraging the rest of them to
flap off in all directions
a feathered stampede

I would have to start again from the beginning
patiently coax one of the mother ducks as leader
hoping to entice them to follow her into the open door
of their duck dormitory

Great-Aunt Delia watched me from the edge of the pond
I was glad she didn't say anything
pleased she understood I needed to find my own way
to do things

this time
they walked calmly into the pen
all fifty of them
like a band marching down main street on Canada Day
proud in their black and white uniforms
nodding graciously at imaginary bystanders
sure of their route and destination
as if they alone had thought to do this

I shut the door quickly
they were safe from harm for the night
safe from death by coyotes

I said to her:
this can be a difficult job sometimes

Great-Aunt Delia said:

"them ducks;
them ducks is like husbands

ornery

and they don't herd worth a darn"

The Speed of Loneliness

she worked hard all her life
married at seventeen to a good man but he is poor
her daughter married and gave birth by fifteen so
at the tender age of thirty three
she becomes a grandmother
looking quite a bit like Demi Moore but heavier
also grumpier because of all the hard work
on the small farm twenty miles from town

they drive into town for groceries and she says Fred
let's go to the movies
I am sick and tired of work
I work all day at the school
all evening for the kids and grandchildren
the house is always full of people and I am tired
tired, tired, tired
school is out for the summer we can go to a movie
have a nice dinner afterwards and then go home

Fred says, no, honeybun, let's not do that
I don't feel like going to the movies
we are going to the hardware store
then to the grocery store
we have to get two fifties of flour for bread at the co-op
some bags of sugar for when the berries ripen
then we are going home
we can have a good supper when we get home

Helen says look:
I went back to school to get my degree
worked my way through University
got a good job at the school
I grow an acre of garden every year
preserve all our food for the winter
I sew all our clothes and I am soon going to be
forty five years old and I am tired

if you won't come to the movies with me
I will go without you

so off she goes with her cousin Cheryl who lives in town
goes to movies all the time
eats in restaurants
never opens a single jar that has
home made food in it because
what's wrong with MacDonald's for heavens sakes

on the way to the theatre
Helen and Cheryl stop at the bar
it is the first time in twenty five years
Helen has had a drink
one cooler and she is off to the races

she doesn't come to until Monday morning where she
finds herself the star of the show with not only one but two
new boyfriends vying for her attention
one of whom wants to marry her and take her back to Vancouver
because, he says: the fragrance of her hair is like that of
wild mountain bluebells

so Helen goes to Vancouver with him but excludes the
getting married, she already being quite firmly married to
Fred, who might raise some objections

she has now been there three months
it is fall and she knows mists are curling up from the
Nechako River near where she used to live
she can feel it in her bones, this mist,
and she longs for it
she misses the silence before the geese start calling
the intense blue of the northern sky
she misses the northern lights, and
her children and grandchildren, but

she has lost thirty pounds and now wears jeans with a
twenty seven inch waistband and bellbottoms
around which are colourful braids embroidered with
flowers, just like the seventies
they make her feel good
like she used to when she was seventeen and
first laid eyes on Fred, the bugger
who was more interested in her bellbottoms being
off than on

she thinks of the garden
how lovingly she planted it this spring

it must be gone to weeds by now but still
there would be enough vegetables to put in the root cellar

she imagines herself filling the bins
carrots, potatoes, beets
the shelves with jars of preserves
and the comfort of seeing one of Fred's moose
quartered, hanging in the ice house

she thinks about her new Vancouver life
her boyfriend whose name is Jason
her size twenty seven inch waist jeans

she drinks a glass of chilled juice
mmmm-mango
wonders if mangoes would grow up north
decides no, they would not grow
no matter what kind of greenhouse you had
they would not grow in the north

she looks at her manicured fingernails
knowing what digging potatoes would do to their
acrylic tips painted a brand new shade called
rapunzel red
she thinks of her new job teaching in a private school
nine to five with a whole hour just for lunch
just for her lunch
eaten at a vegan restaurant
then her daily treat: English Toffee Coffee
size small in a brown paper cup with a java jacket
to carry back to the school for dessert

Fred has called and asked her to come home
come home for the winter, he said, we miss you

she brushes a speck of dust from her tan leather boots
realizing that these boots will never see mud
nor hard work

she stretches her now lean body and says:
no Fred, I am not coming home

you should have come to the movies with me

I told you

Must Be True, It Was In The Newspaper

in London, the Buckingham Palace one, not Ontario
two enterprising persons have founded a new company called
The Nice Factor
specializing in three hundred dollar weekend workshops
teaching people how to stop being excessively nice

sometimes, say their teachers, there is no substitute for
bluntness:
if a bore corners you at a party, just say this:
look! I find what you are saying to be incredibly boring
I am going to talk to someone else now
goodbye!

the founder of The Nice Factor is quoted by Reuters as saying:
"the power structure of the world has
socialized women into being excessively nice
therefore it doesn't surprise me that
ninety percent of my clients are women"

In Germany, as astute business woman has opened
a new business called rent-a-call
for a fee of eight dollars per call
clients who have their own cell phones are supplied with
pre-arranged calls to them while they are waiting in restaurants
attending meetings, waiting in airports or other public places
so they will look and sound important
people observing them will think they are busy, popular, and
very much in demand

when interviewed about the resounding success of her business
the owner of rent-a-call said most of her clients are men

In Prince George today in a small restaurant
the man at the next table received a cell phone call
he was seated less than four feet from my ears
I heard every word he shouted into the cell phone
to someone known to him as Charlie, old buddy
it went on for five minutes
disturbing the peace

I wanted to reach over, say to him:
look! I find what you are saying to be incredibly boring

Legacy

somebody else is driving your
fancy red oldsmobile

a woman with a child and
a small dog
drives slowly past my house
looking at each house number

my heart leapt the first time she drove by
I thought it was you, my dear friend
I wish it were
but I had forgotten for a moment that
you died
in the spring

just when we were going to take that trip
to the mountains
gather wild forget-me-nots
beside the curve in the creek where you
felt sure there were
little people
singing softly under the murmur of the water

then at the old cabin
put the flowers in an empty jam jar
pretend we still had a kitchen table with oilcloth
a woodstove with a big kettle boiling
day and night
a teapot full of black tea
strong enough to skate on

your car has been sold to a woman with
a child and a small dog

---

a new partner now holds the hand of your
husband
lives in your house
reads mail left in
your mailbox
bathes in your jacuzzi

I see them together at the symphony
the theatre
the hockey game

your husband looks tanned and fit
well dressed on the money you left him to
enjoy life despite his grief
over you

I rake up the fall leaves
lean on the rake
watch the driver find her destination

she parks the oldsmobile
takes the child in her arms
closes the car door
walks away from the car

the little dog jumps up and down on the seat
barking in a fury at being

left behind

Chairoscuro: Clear Dark

A Northern Woman

Starlit Nights At Thirty Five Below
   Zero

Flowers The Size Of Dinner Plates

What It Sounds Like

View From His Log House In Winter

Henry Gustafson

Mary MacEwan's Memories Of Johnny
   MacEwan

The Auld Soul

Cooking For The Trophy Hunters

Wholly Communion

Home-made Fish And Chips

A Recipe For Bannock

Cries In The Night

Conversation At Snowshoe Creek

Higher Ground

Mick Mouse

Beautiful Darning Stitches Woven In A
   Circle

Raffle

Chiaroscuro: Clear Dark

A Northern Woman

driving back home to the farm
after celebrating a reunion with
friends in Vancouver
I start to feel different
just after Cache Creek

the feeling is one of extraordinary
certainty as if the road has been
waiting for me
rolling out before me like a
welcome mat
lifting me up plateau by plateau
my spirit rising with the increase in elevation

I stop near Seventy Mile House
where the land spreads out
to accommodate a wider sky, the
deep Cariboo blue the bush pilots call
a blue blazer

I drink tea from the thermos
look around at what city people might think bleak
pine trees, gravel roads
and see only the beauty of it
a place where names on signposts say
Bonaparte River
Buffalo Creek

on through Hundred Mile House
past Lac La Hache all the way to
Williams Lake and then by late afternoon
Quesnel where the highway runs
right through the centre of town

another hour of driving and I'll be in Prince George
still more than one hundred miles from home

at the Mohawk Station
I meet a friend of mine, transporting
his livestock back from the auction
in a long red horse trailer behind
his pickup truck

I tell him about the trip
the sense of heading for somewhere
really special, exciting, not just home but
the unique landscape of the north
as if I am thirsting to be surrounded by
this particular land

yes, he says, I know what you mean
I think about this a lot, how we get
hooked on the north
the rivers, the mountains, the sky
how northern people are so
different from people in other places
but I think it's all about the land
it draws us in, like dreaming
and we grow to love it

it is the land itself that has taught us
to love it
the land doesn't belong to us
we belong to it

Starlit Nights At Thirty Five Below Zero

elephants eat
palm kernels which they
excrete intact

these kernels
drying in the hot African sun
become a form of vegetarian ivory
hard as rock, more accessible
much more practical than
ivory from tusks

mobile ivory factories
roaming lumberingly across the veldt
no labour problems, unions
shareholders' meetings
directors' salaries
deaths

our cattle and horses grew
extra thick hair last fall
they knew a ferociously cold
Canadian winter
was on its way

Flowers The Size of Dinner Plates

last night
the full moon poured
a crescendo of light
down the mountains
through spruce and cedar groves
to the river

today
hundreds of new blossoms
bloom on the pumpkin vines

silken orange chalices
dripping gold dust
petals curled wide in
abandon
trumpet ecstasy
to the morning sun

What It Sounds Like

the word bell signifies too
single a sound to describe your
voice, better to say *carillon*

every evening when I was a
child in Wellington
the harmony of the carillon
filled the streets with
song and melody and now
when I hear you speak
your volume, pitch, timbre
weave their colours into a cloak that
envelops me in the same remembered
mesmerizing music

your voice slows time
takes me away to morning sunlight
warm on an antique cedar table
where a jar of liquid honey
sits too long with the lid off
so that some of it dries, thickens
separates into hundreds of
creamy, oatmeal particles

when the jar is tipped to get
honey rolling onto the spoon
the golden liquid is captured by these
grainy jewels which
impede the speed of the pouring but
move in a gracious, elegant dance

I marvel at the beauty as the sunlight shines
through the flecked golden sweetness
suddenly astonished, humbled, grateful
that there are mountain-sides
covered with wild purple fireweed and
creatures
so amazing as bees

View From His Log House In Winter

he told me that he once saw
one lone coyote running
behind a mule deer
she was bleeding heavily
from wounds on her back legs

running down beside Songere Creek
with the coyote in hot pursuit
she left blood on the snow
a message that read
I am destined to die
I will never leave this valley

down the creek she ran
out onto the frozen river ice
limping
never looking back at the coyote
which had slowed down
aware her lifeblood was pouring out
knowing what the doe knew
that she would soon have
only enough strength to lie down and
hope to die
before the coyote reached her

Henry Gustafsen

was a craggy, rangy fellow
had lived in these mountains all his life
told me he was ninety six years old and
proud to be known as
the biggest liar in the valley so I could
make up my own mind about his age

we walked a couple of miles to look at
a horse he said would be perfect for my
children also very inexpensive
an opportunity I should not miss
a horse so small you could take it home
folded up in the trunk of a car

I was thirty five, he was ninety six
I couldn't keep up to his hiking pace
with my three little ones in tow
he strode off through the bush without me
humming to himself
whistling his own imitations of bird calls

he had caught the horse and put a lead rope
on its halter by the time I arrived to do my
amateur inspection
yes, I said, they will love this gentle creature
I paid him the money, eighty bucks cash
a fortune then
said I would come back when I found
someone to help me transport the horse home

he said: that is no way to do business
I could resell this horse the minute you leave
don't trust the biggest liar in the valley
then he made us a cup of tea
we drank it at his kitchen table
which had a tablecloth made of
old newspapers

henry came along for the ride the day
the horse was trucked to our farm
wanted to see my children's delight
at this horse they had decided to name
"Thunder"

we sat on the riverbank watching them ride
it was a such a bad mosquito day I wore
a head net that covered my face and neck
so they wouldn't drive me nuts with their
whining buzzing kamikaze landings

Henry said look, I have bare arms and
no mosquitos land on me
you are attracting them with all that
slapping them away you are doing
they aren't biting me at all
you have to commune with them
stay calm and peaceful
then they won't bite you
they won't even land on you

I watched carefully and it was true
the mosquitos didn't land on him
but I said: oh sure
and you're the biggest liar in the valley

no, he said, I'm serious, your thoughts about
not liking to be bitten make you agitated and
that affects your body temperature
the mosquitos can sense this change
it tells them where you are
so they can hone in on you
try calmness and acceptance of them
they will no longer bite you
roll up your sleeves and try it

I did what he said
and damned if it didn't work
that was the last summer I ever wore a head net

I worked outdoors all the time after that
wearing no bug dope either and
the mosquitos didn't bother me

honest

Mary MacEwan's Memories Of Johnny MacEwan

my daddy was a logger up in Prince George
some people called them rednecks
rough tough redneck logger

to us four children he used to say:
there's mean times ahead
do your homework

we would pout, complain, in vain
he made us study
forced us to get an education

he didn't live to see his way of life denied
denigrated by people who have mistaken
the enemy, blaming the workers
instead of the money-junkies with their
dividend tax credits and offshore cash who
control it all from behind the scenes
like marionettes with clipboards

I miss those old days
suppertime, Saturday night, pay-day
hockey night in Canada on the radio
kitchen windows all steamed up from
supper cooking on the stove, days when I
used to think everything would be fine

daddy home from work, bearded
beaming at us
snapping his red suspenders
chewing Copenhagen snoose
tired, triumphant
he would put his pay-cheque on the table
say to my mother:

for you my darlin'
everything I have
all for you

The Auld Soul

my son is living on the streets now
she says
there ain't a damn thing I can do to change it

she fills the kettle
turns off the tap with
measured determined firm twists
something dependable
predictable

you turn the tap clockwise
it closes

last time he came home
she says
he seemed more peaceful
brought a new friend along
a tiny person named Betty who
listened to him
looked at him with respect
they went for long walks together
out in the bush, down to the lake

I prayed they would stay here for a while but
suddenly there was a wild fever in his eyes and
he had to leave

the kettle whistles
her strong arms lift it from the woodstove
she pours steaming water into a
big brown teapot and says:
Betty told me later he cried when he saw the clearcuts
saw the forest was gone from the hillsides
he made wailing sounds
howled at the sky
shaking his fists in despair

Betty said:
he went ballistic

I remember him when he was five
we were working on our fence lines
removing small trees and brush
that could push the fence wires down or
knock over the posts as they grew
we called this *mending fence*
to keep our cattle in

he went ballistic that day too
he had never seen anyone cut trees

five years old
he threw himself on the ground
kicking, furious
then he got up and ran at my friend
who was holding the chain saw
tears pouring down his little face he screamed:

"leave them alone! leave them alone!
they are *my* trees
they are *my* trees"

Cooking For The Trophy Hunters

well it's a job, very close to home
my children can come to work with me
we can trail across the fields at six a.m
to the cabin where the hunters stay with the
big game guide
earn money I wouldn't otherwise have
even if it is only ten bucks a day
cooking on a three burner coleman stove
by the light of a kerosene lantern

the hunters are from the states
courtly men, old fashioned, respectful to me
in my jac shirt and boots as I carry firewood
inside for the woodstove
they call me ma'am which sounds wonderful
in their slow and lyrical way of speaking
until I realize its easier than remembering my name
or regarding me as an individual

for their dinner
I cook sautéed morel mushrooms
arrange them in circles on the moose steaks

one man from Texas says: where's the ketchup

there is none, I say, we don't serve ketchup on
morel mushrooms they are so delicate
so fragrant they need to be eaten without condiments
try these steamed fiddlehead ferns with them

ma'am, he says, where's the ketchup

I repeat my defence of the morels to no avail
this charming man is actually quite upset
although still calling me ma'am, spoken with an
implied little bow with each use of the word

he says: pass me the ketchup
or we'll just get our own from our vee-hickle

I say look, we don't have any ketchup
it is not something we use in this kitchen
we just don't have any ketchup, that's all

he sends his friend Bob outside to their
camper vehicle parked under the trees nearby
and Bob returns triumphant

all of them are very pleased to see the ketchup
their faces light up
they greet the ketchup like an old friend

they up-end the bottle in turns
hammer the end of it with the heel of their hand
pour it out over their steak and mushrooms

I watch the mushrooms disappear under a sea of red
think of the time it took us to pick them
the effort we made to contribute
something unique, locally grown
to celebrate their stay in the mountains

they have done me a favour
my workdays will be easier from now on
they want bacon and eggs for breakfast
sandwiches made with mayo and hot dogs
for their carry out lunch
dinner will be easy: fry the steaks when
I hear their riverboat pull in at the landing
put their massive bottle of ketchup on the table
dish out mashed spuds, peas, and canned corn

after they finish eating
I will wash up the dishes in the
red and white oval enamel dishpan
then hotfoot it back across the field
joyfully home to our house
where the children and I will dine on
steamed fiddleheads with nutmeg
fresh trout, sautéed morel mushrooms
and wild blueberries

Wholly Communion

a lot of houses are backwards with their
oppressive picture windows
long bleak living rooms
warren-like bedrooms
tiny kitchens with
no soul, no passion, in them

give me a big kitchen twenty feet wide and
thirty feet long
and right bang in the middle
a wide cedar plank table
where great numbers of us can gather
in celebration or sorrow
companionable silence or
riotous song and laughter

daybed beside the brick chimney
soup simmering on the antique cookstove
skimmed milk warming for yoghurt
sourdough whole wheat bread rising
everything organic, locally grown, homemade

a narrow pantry the length of the room
doors you can fold back and find everything
just where you left it
thirty feet of visible storage space
plates and bowls and knives and forks
grains and herbs and spices
jars of garden preserves
standing in rows of vibrant colour
witness to our gratitude to the summer earth

we can sit and talk while we
shell peas or shuck corn
prepare food for the winter
mix up fruit for a wedding cake
prepare sustenance for a funeral
write words in icing sugar on birthday cakes or
share pot luck suppers with friends who bring

unique creations of their own design
arugula and coriander with raspberries
brown rice noodles with walnuts and olive oil
red onion, orange and blueberry salad
mustard beans and lentil dhal

food prepared with respect
carried with love and ceremony in thick
pottery dishes to the plain wooden table

and while we are all gathered at the table
talking planning composing laughing
nourishing ourselves and each other
there would still be space for little children to
run around behind us in a circle
until they get tired then
lie down under the table
close enough to hear our voices
our stories

or curl up in our lap
listening to our heart beat

Home-made Fish And Chips

ling cod have very slimy skin
thick, viscous, disagreeable

on the side of the garage there is a
six inch nail hammered in half way
at just the right height to hang a ling cod
by the gills so we can
slit the skin around the neck
grip the edges of the skin with the
black handled pliers
and slowly, carefully, gently
pull the skin down the
body of the fish right to its tail

once the ling has been skinned
we chop off the tail, remove the head
and our fresh fish is ready to cook for supper

we save the skin, the head, and the guts
bury them deep in the garden to enrich the soil

the children take turns with the skinning
its an adventure they enjoy
a challenge to get the skin to curl just right
so it will slip off easily

when they do it well
when the whole skin slips down in one piece
it makes them feel triumphant

one day I stand in the sunshine thinking
how odd to be watching the children so
completely absorbed in this
merciless fish skinning ritual
with a pair of black pliers that used to
have such a genteel life

my mother used them for
gardening tasks in New Zealand
securing labels on rose bushes
twisting delicate florists' wire
to hold exotic plants in place

I inherited them
always carried them with me
in my travelling days
to adjust bindings on my skis or
make small repairs on suitcase locks
I wonder what she would think as we
use them to skin a five pound ling cod to
feed her never-seen grandchildren

especially if she could see
how perfectly those pliers fit into
three pairs of small hands
with fingers that are square shaped
like hers, like mine

A Recipe For Bannock

take some flour and a pinch of salt
a teaspoonful of baking powder
a little wheat germ and bran
some powdered milk
put it in a brown paper bag and shake it up
ready to carry down to the river in your
backpack with swimsuits, towels, some
wild raspberry jam, butter, matches, band-aids
one spoon, one knife, one bowl for mixing

walking in the sunshine through the forest
your guitar slung over your shoulder
you stop to look at damp mossy glades where your
three small children can imagine
worlds within worlds
under the waving fronds of
two inch high mosses

imagine fairies winged and unwinged
swathed in tulle
dancing arabesques
their minute toes *en pointe*

imagine miniscule elves in green caps reciting
"I am the merry wanderer of the night!
I dance to Oberon and make him laugh."
to an audience of undersized elders who
recline on chairs made of tiny blossoms
and oh, over here, look, small people are
sweeping little doorsteps or
gathering dewdrops
in lily-of-the-valley cups

you sit for an hour while the children
tell their stories, name their imaginary people
build family trees of connections
gently touch the hard curled edges of the lichen on
surrounding rocks and stones or admire the
sponginess and intricate patterns of the moss
exclaiming over the colours and shapes of
tiny flowers that peek through it
like hidden jewels suddenly revealed

the holiness to this part of the journey changes
the minute you arrive at the swimming pool
between the island and the hayfield

reverence changes to exuberance as they
shriek and swim and jump into the water
playing their invented games
slathering themselves with river silt
washing it off, then re-applying the dark mud
covering themselves so they can
wash it off again

"look at me, Mum" they shout with
each costume change

on the stones beside the river
you build a small fire
grease the whittled sticks
cached under the picnic table
mix up the bannock with some water
wind the dough around the sticks
making sure it covers the end so there will be
one end open and one closed
like a long cave

place the bannock gently on the fire to
cook in the embers

when the children tire of swimming in the
clear cold mountain water
the bannock is ready
it slips off the stick leaving a place for
home made butter and wild raspberry jam

your fingers covered in charred black crumbs and
bright red succulent juice
you and your children eat bannock
beside a campfire
where the Smoky River
only a trickle at the Great Divide
pours turquoise water
into the Fraser River at Crescent Island

afterwards, the children sing along while you
strum chords on the guitar
the midnight special, the sloop john b,
row your boat, springtime in the rockies,
the skye boat song, pokare kare ana,
puff the magic dragon

the walk home seems
ten times as long as the journey down
going back on the road beside the river

this valley between the Rockies and the
Snowshoe and Cariboo Mountains is bathed in the
purples, yellows, and reds of the setting sun

you and your children will
sleep the sweet sleep of
physical exhaustion tonight

there are other recipes for bannock
this is my favourite

Cries In The Night – Part One

this is how it works:
one lone coyote walks out of the bush
stands in the clearing that surrounds the house
our dog runs toward the coyote, barking
the coyote retreats back into the bush
the dog goes back to her doghouse

the coyote reappears
coming not quite so close this time

the dog makes another advance
to show who is boss
runs even further away from
her safety zone

the coyote retreats
the dog goes back to lie down
the coyote reappears

each time this happens
the dog is enticed closer to the bush until
she is barking at not just one coyote but
a whole pack of them
assembled just inside the edge of the bush
waiting for her

Cries In The Night – Part Two

when the coyotes were around
they kept us awake
yipping and crying

we tied our dog up
close to the house every night

one night we erred on the side of kindness
thinking the coyotes had moved on
let her run free
when we got up in the morning
she was gone

at seven thirty, when I stood at the door
watching my children walk
up the Cranberry path to the schoolbus
Chris called out to me:
Mum, it's Brandy
they got her, she's dead
can you come and get her so I don't
miss the bus

he had found her on the train tracks
didn't think it was her at first
so small, so light, so frail

as I ran toward him
I watched him move her off the tracks
he didn't want her run over by a train
on top of being killed by the coyotes

he sent Dan and Morgen ahead to
ask the driver to hold the bus for him
took her in his arms
placed her lovingly in the long grass

then he dusted himself off
picked up his books, his lunchkit
and ran up the hill

at the top he turned around to
watch me carry Brandy back home

silent, we looked long at one another
I will never forget the expression on his face
responsibility, regret, love, anguish, trust

Conversation At Snowshoe Creek

he is riding Dusty, the buckskin mare
six miles down the gravel road

at Snowshoe Creek, the old bridge has been
reconstructed with new bridge timbers

they spook her as she steps on them, they
make the rushing water sound strange to her
it echoes differently from before
she does not feel secure on the new surface
everything seems frightening
she balks and will not cross

he dismounts and soothes the mare
speaks to her quietly
holding the reins in one hand
massaging her neck with the other
then remounts and tries to ride her across
she refuses, rears up on her hind legs
backs herself off the timbered surface
stands still on safe ground on the gravel road

he dismounts again and stands close to her
speaks to her, rubs her neck and her ears
then leads her across the bridge
reins loosely held, walking slowly
she follows him to the other side

instead of mounting the horse
continuing on his way
he leads her gently back across the bridge
back to the starting point then across again

he does this five times
praising her when they reach the other side
talking to her all the time
calming her

only then does he climb back into the saddle
ride her across the bridge
back and forth several times
to make sure she is comfortable
before going on his way

he doesn't know that from the
only dwelling on this lonely road
he is being observed through the trees
by Alf and his wife Dot who are
having afternoon tea
at the window of their cabin

he is my son
his name is Danny
he is twelve years old
it was Alf and Dot who told me this story
Danny never mentioned it

Higher Ground

early springtime
still four or five feet of snow on the ground
my son was working miles up Pass Lake Road
almost to the Herrick Valley
running survey lines among old spruce trees

preparatory work that could lead eventually to
no old-growth trees living in this forest
everything clearcut and hauled away by the
timber companies

hard going in snowshoes
on grainy spring snow
each granule heavy with water

a six kilometer walk uphill to the site
then running the deflection line
up the middle of the cut-block to the top
while his partner marked the boundary lines

on the way there in the morning
he fell into the river
wrung his clothes out and continued on

he had seen a male grizzly
two days before in the same area
man and grizzly stared at one another until
the bear decided to turn back into the bush

in town that night the boss insisted
cans of bear spray must be
attached to their vests at all times

he thought he would never use it
he had grown up in bear country
frightened them away with bear bangers

he tied the can of bear spray to his vest

at lunchtime he found a dry spot
under a spruce where the snow had begun
to melt away from the dark perimeter of the trunk
settled in to eat his sandwich and rest

in a clearing forty metres downhill
he saw a mother grizzly sniffing the air

when she reared up on her hind legs
his sinking heart knew she had found him
she charged toward him
her twin two-year-old cubs following

to his surprise time seemed to stand still
it stretched to contain all of his thoughts
he became an observer of his own reactions to
her beauty, her colour, her size
a good seven or eight hundred pounds
he admired how fiercely she protected her young
noticed the way the brown of her fur was tipped
with thick ginger streaks

the speed at which she ran
up the thirty five percent incline
filled him with wonder

he thought: this is their home, not ours
it is they who belong here in this
timber and thick undergrowth
the forest should be left alone
so they can live here in peace
he felt like an imposter, an invader

reaching into his vest pocket for his bear banger
he discovered he had lost it
he tried yelling at them to frighten them away
they paid no attention
the sow heading straight for him

he didn't want to use the mace but
she was almost on top of him
he had backed up to the tree trunk
she had to slow down a little to get close to him
he ripped the can from his vest
popped the safety cap
waited until the last minute to spray her

it put her down instantly
stunned by the effects of it, disoriented
puffing, unable to breathe
she batted at her eyes with her paws
attempting to flee from the cloud of mace
she turned away from him
then began to retreat

the two cubs had been standing, waiting
off to one side while she made her attack
then followed her as she left
he knew he was still in grave danger
he feared she would return to attack him again
there was nothing he could do

when he could no longer hear their sounds
he headed downhill to the river

on the drive home
he called me on his radio phone
said he had encountered a grizzly
that she had made a run at him

I went over to his house
stopped at the liquor store on the way
bought a bottle of champagne

we didn't wait to chill it properly
the hell with decorum
we upended it
shared its sparkly sweetness
toasted life
toasted one another

after a while
I asked him

how close?

he said:

about ten inches
a foot maybe at the most
from her claw marks
to the end of my snowshoes

Mick-Mouse

two, four and six years old
they were little buggers at bedtime
I had to bathe them quickly,
one after another
keep the woodstove going full bore
to warm their pyjamas
boil water for hot water bottles

they invented a game which involved
exuberant running totally naked
through the drafty house chasing one another
repeatedly shouting the words
mick-mouse mick-mouse mick-mouse
in the tones of someone announcing
the progress of a horse race
laughing their heads off
running up and down the stairs
through all the rooms
shrieking as loudly as possible

this rousing game of starkers mick-mouse
was their protocol
before consenting to settle down for our
bed-time story rituals

when they grew a little older, lost interest
became too modest to play mick-mouse
I was surprised at how much I missed
watching them running, darting out of my reach
absorbed in the mischievous glee
the triumph
of exasperating their mother

\
years later when they were grown up
living in the city I said to a visiting Chris
as he sat in sunshine at the dining room table
eating breakfast and reading the paper
what is your brother up to this weekend
what is keeping our Danno so occupied?

he looked up and quietly said
don't ask, Mum, I think he might be busy
playing mick-mouse

Beautiful Darning Stitches Woven In A Circle

in January, my daughter was
travelling in New Zealand's summer
kayaking down twenty foot waterfalls and
walking in the footsteps of her Oamaru
ancestors, meeting her relatives
for the first time

at my grandparents' old house
my cousin Sonny Macaulay said:
look Morgen, up the hill behind the house
those are the pine trees your mother heard
singing, when she was just a wee girl

on a tour of Bob Macaulay's garden, Bob
spoke slowly these words of welcome:

you cannot imagine
how long I have waited
to meet you

in Tauranga, she performed a ceremony
of love and remembrance at
my mother's grave
cleaned moss from the headstone
placed flowers, mourned the loss of
a grandmother known only through
stories, reminiscences
and her awareness of my lifelong grief

she brought back to Canada
a photo of the headstone

a distinct image of my daughter
standing in the Tauranga sunshine
taking the picture
is reflected on the shiny marble surface
beside my mother's name

Raffle

in the Spruceland parking lot
two cheerful gentlemen
are selling five dollar tickets for a
shiny tangerine 1940
Plymouth four seater

people crowd around
amazed by the luxury of the
sixty three year old snazzy sports sedan
in perfect condition with a
souped up engine, previously
say the gentlemen
owned by a biker who
spared no expense restoring this
gem he named
"Rita Hayworth"

if the biker remembers Rita
wearing that slinky tangerine dress on
billboard ads for the movie *Gilda*
circa 1956
he must be a fairly agéd biker

I would love to own that car
drive it to the beach
with my three small children
buy them ice cream cones
turn on the radio and sing along with
Abba
but its too late I keep forgetting they are
grown up and gone
damn

well maybe I could go pick up the biker
hello, I won your car
wanna come to the beach?
park in the moonlight?
we could belt out a chorus or two of
"Put The Blame on Mame, Boy"

Chiaroscuro: "Clear Dark"

camping in the mountains
sleeping bags set up in the tent
kettle boiling on the campfire for
a cup of hot rum before bedtime
we are hoping for northern lights

we watch the steam billow up
disappear into the midnight sky

he tells me when he lived in Yellowknife
he heard a legend about Aurora Borealis:
if you whistle up to the lights
they will descend to greet the earth

we wonder if the steam will have
the same effect
we sip our drinks and talk
I tell him about my friend who believes
the objective of life is to turn
sorrows into joys

the northern lights start flashing their
startling contrasts of red and green
fast moving arcs and pillars of
white appear, then fade

subtle gradations of light and shade
shift into rippling curtains of
blues, purples and pinks

we lie on our backs
side by side, looking up

watching the sky bringing
heaven to earth
